THE WORRY (*Less*) JOURNAL

THE WORRY (Less) JOURNAL

Creative Exercises and Mindfulness Practices to Silence Negative Thinking and Find Peace

ERIKA STRAUB MA, BA, RYT

ILLUSTRATIONS BY HANS BENNEWITZ

ROCKRIDGE PRESS

First Rockridge Press trade paperback edition
May 2022

Rockridge Press and the Rockridge Press logo are trademarks or registered trademarks of Callisto Media Inc. and/or its affiliates in the United States and other countries and may not be used without written permission.

For general information on our other products and services, please contact our Customer Care Department within the United States at (866) 744-2665, or outside the United States at (510) 253-0500.

ISBN: 978-1-638-78296-4

Manufactured in the United States of America

Interior and Cover Designer: Lisa Forde
Art Producer: Samantha Ulban
Editor: Mary Colgan
Production Editor: Ashley Polikoff

Illustrations © 2022 Hans Bennewitz. Author Photo Courtesy of Arielle Knapp

10 9 8 7 6 5 4 3 2 1

THIS JOURNAL BELONGS TO

_____

INTRODUCTION

y intention for *The Worry (Less) Journal* is for it to be a resource that you keep in your back pocket and use any time you feel worried. The exercises in this journal will help you change your mindset and increase your sense of awareness within your body. My hope is that this journal will help untether you from the past and increase your confidence that positive outcomes are possible in the future.

Worry robs you of fully experiencing the present moment by seducing you to live in your head. Through intentional practices such as mindfulness and resourcing exercises, you can learn how to quiet your mind and relax your body so you can sink into the moment rather than abandon it by way of worry.

As a trauma and anxiety coach, nervous system expert, and someone who has worked with many clients who deeply struggled with worry, I'm certain that, with the right support, you can transform dysregulation (worry) into regulation (safety). Inner turmoil that once made you feel overwhelmed can become an invitation to self-care and transformation.

I remember working with a client who was plagued by the uncertainty of the future and simultaneously terrified of the past repeating itself. The oscillation between past and future events, the heightened internal pace of their body and mind, and the repetitive playing out of worst-case scenarios rushed them into impulsivity, self-sabotage, and a preoccupation with preparation that didn't allow them to move forward in any facet of their life.

Through understanding their nervous system, equipping themselves with more awareness, resolving underlying trauma, and incorporating the exact tools referenced in this journal, they were able to regulate the worry energy in their body and direct it toward their goals and dreams. They were able to slow down and trust the process, timing, and unfolding of their life.

Healing worry will encourage slowness and presence, and it will help you build enough resilience to move through challenges with more grace and ease.

Understanding Worry

Worry is a combination of thoughts, emotions, sensations, and behaviors that direct your attention toward what could go wrong. It's a survival response to internal discomfort, overwhelm, and fear that is stored within the body. Worry is an evolutionary function—one of the nervous system's best attempts to help you find safety. Unfortunately, the safety that is sought through worrying cannot be found by way of control, predicting and preparing for catastrophes, or overthinking.

Worry isolates you from the present and transports you into past experiences or future possibilities. It invites you to experience life through the mind rather than the body. When worry distracts you from the gravity of the present moment, mindfully inhabiting your body, and tapping into the stillness of your mind, it can lead to continual disembodiment, hypervigilance, and residual fear.

Hypervigilance means you're living in a constant cognitive state of risk analysis, strategizing, evaluating potential threats, catastrophizing worst-case scenarios, and weighing potential consequences.

Within worry are the feelings of anticipation, disquiet, stress, fear, dread, and unease. Worry is also a component of anxiety. Anxiety is characterized by severe and persistent worry that is not proportionate to the situation at issue, leading to extreme avoidance.

While worry can be experienced acutely—especially alongside our natural stress response cycle that mobilizes our survival instincts in the face of danger or challenges—excessive worry debilitates and extinguishes your vitality, spontaneity, and inner peace. Your body and mind lose the ability to rest, leaving you in a state of stimulated exhaustion. Excessive worry feels like the gas and brake pedals being slammed down at the same time, incessantly creating internal havoc and escalating discomfort, which ultimately leads to anxiety.

To ease worry, you first need to learn how to regulate your nervous system, quiet your mind, and feel the emotions and sensations within your body.

Worry and Your Body

Worry affects not only the mind but also the body. While it feels as if you cannot get out of your head when you're worried, you're often already out of your body.

Worry begins in the body, but as the sensations in the body become too uncomfortable, you resort to living in your head. Unfortunately, it's this very experience of disembodiment that leads to further discomfort, disease, and symptom amplification.

When someone experiences acute worry, common symptoms include an accelerated heart rate, perspiration, dizziness, nausea, headaches, impaired sleep, constriction in the body, and the onset of digestive disturbances.

Chronic worry brings with it the possibility for adrenal fatigue, high blood pressure, IBS, ulcers, insomnia, panic attacks, dissociation, depression and anxiety, heart disease, diabetes, asthma, obesity, and more.

It's imperative to learn how to feel the sensations in your body when you're worried. It's only through embodiment that you can change the trajectory of worry, reduce symptoms, and prevent stress-related disease.

Worry and Your Emotions

There is a cognitive, somatic, emotional, and behavioral component to excessive worry. The emotional component to worry is regarding the feelings worry initiates within you. Worry is the primary emotion, yet there are secondary emotions that accompany it. Feelings such as fear, dread, anger, and sadness are a few of the emotions that may be present for you when you're worried.

It's the repetitive nature of worry that results in the decline of emotional well-being and a further disconnect between body and mind. When you're worried, your mind is far from still, quiet, or calm. You can get stuck in a redundant thought loop and feel anxious, depressed, burnt out, fatigued, out of control, and paralyzed by excessive worry.

It's challenging to feel present and emotionally available under these circumstances. Your energy is depleted by trying to manage the thoughts and emotions that worry encompasses.

You may feel trapped by your worries, but worry is an experience you can interrupt by creating a foundation of emotional safety through learning to name, soothe, and honor your feelings.

Worry and Your Social Life

Worry not only impacts your relationship with yourself, but it also impacts your relationship to everything around you. Worry draws you inward, distancing you from the consistency of daily routines as well as the joy of movement and activities, and it can negatively impact your relationships.

One of the most debilitating side effects of worry is the lack of forward progression. The redundancy of worry invites procrastination over simple tasks, produces self-doubt at every interval of action, and manufactures overthinking and indecisiveness. Without consistency of routine or the capacity to create structure, the chaos that ensues due to worry erodes experiences, accomplishments, and creativity.

In relationships, worry becomes a third entity in the dynamic. The circular, repetitive nature of worry stalls a deepening of intimacy. And while relationships aren't perfectly linear, they do have a natural way of unfolding that gets interrupted by worry. Worry calls your attention to what could go wrong, as opposed to what could go right. Worry invalidates integrity, trust, and connection through continuous questioning, hesitation, and need for reassurance that can never be satisfied enough.

You can be in connection, or you can be in protection. Worry requires you to continually guard yourself from other people and the world around you.

Journal Your Worries Away

To interrupt the repetitive nature of worry and create more peace, you can implement intentional practices.

Worry is an unconscious and impulsive habit that began as a coping mechanism to protect you. Unfortunately, the protection that worry offers is limited, because no matter how many worst-case scenarios you fret over, or how long you spend attempting to control the outcomes, worry doesn't create more predictability. Worry only creates disconnection and discomfort.

Because worry is a habit, it can be unlearned and replaced by new habits that serve you. First, you must create more cognitive awareness of your worry. Journaling is one of the ways you can do this. It will reveal to you the roots of your worry so you can better understand it.

Next, you need to expand your body awareness around worry. Mindfulness practices will invite you into the physical sensations of worry that live within your body. Learning how to soothe your body will help you quiet your mind.

And lastly, implementing tools when you feel worried will help you be in relationship to your worry, as opposed to being hijacked by it. The right tools will allow you to witness and listen to your worries, pacify the thoughts and sensations, and settle into more peace in the present moment.

How to Use This Journal

This journal is meant to meet you where you are on your journey with healing worry. Sometimes management tools for worry are needed in the moment, and other times you'll need preventative practices for worry. This journal will provide both.

The Worry (Less) Journal is a supportive resource that can be used as a daily practice, a weekly check-in, or a go-to tool in times of worry. This is not a one-size-fits-all type of journal and doesn't need to be worked through in chronological order. You have the freedom to approach this journal in a way that feels most supportive for you.

The purpose of the creative prompts in this journal is to build a well-rounded tool kit for reducing worry, releasing negative thoughts and emotions, reconnecting your body and mind, and ultimately, to help you find more inner peace.

Here are the elements of the journal and how to engage with them:

Affirmations are mantras that can help you challenge negative thoughts and overcome self-sabotaging behaviors. You can use affirmations in any situation where you'd like to see a positive change.

Writing prompts will help you get your thoughts down on paper and guide you in reflecting on topics such as how you process emotions, how you relate to fear, what you worry about, and what positive possibilities the future holds.

Creative prompts are meant to help you tap into your creativity and self-expression. These prompts will inspire you to implement art and imagination to engage and connect with all parts of yourself.

Mindfulness practices will help you be more present and aware of your body and emotions.

Exercises are interactive activities that will provoke new perspectives, help you break old patterns, and invite you into deeper self-inquiry.

Sometimes it's challenging to engage with new practices, and you'll want to resort to old ways of being with your worry. Give yourself grace as you walk through this transformation. Move at a pace that is comfortable and supportive based on your needs. You know yourself best.

This journal is not intended to be a substitute for therapy, medication, or other professional treatments for excessive worry. Seek assistance from a mental health professional if your symptoms linger or begin to overwhelm your life.

Worry is meant to show you parts of yourself that need healing. It's not a life sentence; you just need the right support and tools.

IT'S SAFE TO FEEL MY EMOTIONS. IT'S SAFE TO FEEL SENSATIONS IN MY BODY.

1

Imagine worry is a person you want to get to know. Describe how worry looks, how worry thinks and feels, what worry wants and needs, and if worry has anything to share with you.

_____

_____

_____

_____

_____

_____

_____

_____

_____

_____

_____

_____

Behind worry is a massive amount of tension in your body, some of which you might not even be aware of. When your body experiences such a high level of tension, it often goes numb as a way to protect you from pain and discomfort. This is a great short-term strategy, but when it becomes chronic, you end up living in a state of numbness and autopilot.

If there is tension in the body, it will be very difficult, if not impossible, to release yourself from worry. Helping your body relax will relax your mind, too.

1. Grab a tennis ball, lacrosse ball, softball, or foam roller. Place it on the ground and lay the part of your body that has the most tension on top of it.

2. As you roll this part of your body over the ball or foam roller, you will feel the discomfort of the knotted tension within your body. It won't feel good in the moment.

3. Breathe through the sensations you are feeling.

4. When you stand up, notice how you feel in your body.

Emotions are messengers that deliver insights to you about yourself. Sometimes you have to learn how to speak their language so you can understand what they're trying to convey.

Worry is a collection of a few different emotions. If each of these emotions had a voice, what would they say? Would you be willing to listen? Fill in the table with the message communicated by each of the following emotions.

EMOTION	MESSAGE
Anger	
Fear	
Sadness	
Anxiety	
Worry	
Hypervigilance	

Who did you witness being worried when you were growing up? How did they behave, talk, or maybe even change when they were worried? How did it make you feel?

_____

_____

_____

_____

_____

_____

_____

_____

_____

_____

_____

Think of five things you associate with feeling calm, such as the sound of
ocean waves or the smell of baking cookies. Write one on each of the fingers of the
illustration. On the palm, draw a picture of a scene you find calming.

Music directly influences your mood. Your music preferences develop based on how songs make you feel. We often select music that matches how we're feeling. Have you ever reflected on how a song feels in your body?

1. Choose three songs from different genres.

2. Find a comfortable place to sit down and close your eyes.

3. Listen to one song all the way through and note how it makes you feel in your body.

4. Repeat this exercise for the next two songs. Compare how each song felt within your body.

Identify a worry thought. See if you can find facts and clues to dispute this thought. Next, replace the thought with a more realistic self-statement. Repeat this exercise for five different worry thoughts and notice how finding facts to counter your worry helps reduce it.

WORRY THOUGHT	FACTS AND CLUES TO DISPUTE IT	REALISTIC SELF-STATEMENT

I MAY NOT
BE ABLE TO
CHOOSE MY
THOUGHTS, BUT
I CAN CHOOSE
WHAT THOUGHTS
I BELIEVE.

Is worry something you can take responsibility for, or is worry the fault of someone else?

_____

_____

_____

_____

_____

_____

_____

_____

_____

_____

_____

When you're worried, one thought leads to another and another.
Before you know it, your thoughts are racing, and you feel like you're spiraling.
It's easy to take your worried thoughts at face value. While you can't choose
your thoughts, you can choose which ones you believe. Use the illustration to identify
your default thought when you're worried. Track the thought after that, and
so on. For each worried thought, ask yourself if it's true and if you have to believe it.
Worry loses its power when you don't believe your worried thoughts.

WHEN I NOTICE
MY MIND IS LOUD,
I CAN SLOW MY
BODY DOWN
TO QUIET MY
THOUGHTS.

When you feel worried, you may notice that your breath is shallow. The inhale becomes more active, and the exhale becomes shorter and more passive. A long deep exhale soothes the nervous system and helps you feel calm. Practicing the "voo" breath is one way to bring mindfulness to your breathing and quiet your worries.

1. Find a comfortable place to sit on the floor with your back up against the wall.

2. Bring one hand to your heart and the other to your stomach.

3. Gently inhale through your nose.

4. As you exhale, purse your lips and make the sound *voo*. Try to extend the sound for as long as you still have breath. You will feel the vibrational sound of *voo* beneath your palms. The vibration will release any tension in your body and allow you to take a deeper, fuller breath.

5. Repeat for five breaths at a time as often as needed.

Recall a time you felt worried and were soothed or supported by another person. What happened? How did you feel before and after receiving support?

_____

_____

_____

_____

_____

_____

_____

_____

_____

_____

_____

_____

Use words or pictures to deposit all your worries in the
worry jar. Imagine placing this jar somewhere in your house for safekeeping.
You can open the worry jar at a later time and then put it
back. You are in control of how much you allow yourself to worry.

I CAN DO
HARD THINGS
SOFTLY.

Excessive worry involves repetitively going over a thought or a problem without ever finding a solution. To create more inner peace, excessive worry needs to be transformed into problem-solving. Problem-solving entails finding solutions to difficult or complex issues. Name one situation in your life right now that you keep replaying in your mind. Then, identify five steps you could take that would help you reach a solution, thereby reducing your worry.

Situation you're ruminating on: _____

_____

Action steps:

1. _____

2. _____

3. _____

4. _____

5. _____

IT'S SAFE TO SLOW DOWN. IT'S SAFE TO LET GO. IT'S SAFE TO JUST BE.

Do you ever feel a sense of gratitude for your worry? Is there something you've learned about yourself through the experience of feeling worried?

_____

_____

_____

_____

_____

_____

_____

_____

_____

_____

_____

Worry can manifest as tension in your body. You can invite the tension to let go by contracting and relaxing your muscles in connection with your breath. When you let go of tension, you let go of worry.

1. Find a quiet space where you feel safe.

2. Lie down and gently close your eyes.

3. Notice your breath and the tension (or lack of tension) within your body without trying to change or fix it.

4. Bring awareness to your feet.

5. As you inhale through your nose, squeeze your toes and contract the soles of your feet. Hold the contraction as you hold your breath.

6. As you exhale through your mouth, slowly release the tension within your toes and feet.

7. Continue upward through your body, contracting and relaxing the muscles of the lower legs, then the upper legs, the stomach, back, chest, arms, and face.

8. Take one final inhale as you contract your entire body, and exhale slowly as you release, muscle by muscle.

I CHOOSE TO
HONOR HOW I
FEEL AND WHAT
I NEED. IT IS
SAFE TO PUT
MYSELF FIRST.

Emotions aren't like light switches that you can turn on and off.
They are more like dimmers. Imagine you feel calm and joyful at the brightest setting.
Add words or pictures to the scene to show how that feels in the room.

Before you felt worried, there was something that caused it. Being able to identify triggers will help you prevent worry.

Something also helped you get to the other side of your worry and feel more relaxed. Being able to identify what helped you will reduce your worry.

Identify five times that you felt worried in the last few months. Then note the trigger of each worry and name the tool that helped you get to the other side of each worry.

WORRY	TRIGGER	TOOL

Do you often feel a sense of urgency, desperation, or the pressure of something being time sensitive? Is the feeling based on facts or is it simply a feeling?

_____

_____

_____

_____

_____

_____

_____

_____

_____

_____

_____

_____

REST IS
PRODUCTIVE.
I CAN REST MY
BODY TO REST
MY MIND.

This exercise is about how it feels rather than how it looks. Shaking the body helps reset the nervous system and release tension and worry energy.

1. In the privacy of your own space, start by standing evenly on both feet.

2. Stretch your arms out in front of you and then out to the sides, making sure you have enough room to move freely.

3. Set a timer for two minutes.

4. Start by making small bouncing movements in your lower body and shaking out your hands.

5. Allow this movement to get bigger until your entire body is engaged in movement and shaking.

6. After two minutes, slowly return to stillness and take an inventory of how you feel.

7. Repeat this exercise three times, making sure to return to stillness between each shaking practice.

What are some ways you can take care of yourself when you feel worried?

_____

_____

_____

_____

_____

_____

_____

_____

_____

_____

I AM
NOT ALONE,
I AM
WITH MYSELF.

In the midst of worry, you must learn to stay and let the storm pass by. You learn to become an anchor. What is a thought that will help anchor you when you feel worried? Write down your anchoring message and repeat it as often as needed.

Focusing on a single object will help focus your mind. You will be able to notice what is right in front of you rather than focusing on the past or the future. Grab one object in your home. It can be anything from a coffee mug to a candle. This object may be very familiar to you, but you may have never taken the time to actually notice it. Write down ten observations about the object. When you hone your focus, notice how much you've reduced your worry.

1. _____

2. _____

3. _____

4. _____

5. _____

6. _____

7. _____

8. _____

9. _____

10. _____

Write a letter to yourself from your worry. What does worry want to tell you? What message does your worry have for you?

_____

_____

_____

_____

_____

_____

_____

_____

_____

_____

_____

_____

THIS IS
HAPPENING FOR
ME, NOT TO ME.
BEST-CASE
SCENARIOS
ARE JUST AS
POSSIBLE.

Write a wish for yourself on each star.

When you feel worried, you're not actually present. You're in your head and not in your body. You're disconnected from the moment and the surrounding environment.

To interrupt the vortex of worry thought loops, you must come back to the present, to your environment, and to your body by engaging your senses.

1. Look around your environment and name five things that you see.

2. Scan your environment and listen, and name four sounds you hear.

3. Touch three places on your body and notice the sensations.

4. Name two things you smell.

5. Lastly, name one thing you taste.

Engaging with your senses brings you back to the here and now, breaking the worry thought patterns. Worry and presence cannot exist together.

IT, TOO,
SHALL PASS.
FEELINGS ARE
TEMPORARY. I
CAN STAY AS THE
STORM PASSES.

Worry is often felt alongside other emotions. Slowing down and naming these emotions can prevent worry from escalating. Describe other emotions you experience when you feel worried.

_____

_____

_____

_____

_____

_____

_____

_____

_____

_____

_____

When you feel worried, sometimes it just feels like too much, and you need another person's help to calm down—someone with whom you feel comfortable. Check off the top ten most important qualities you seek in others before you feel comfortable sharing your worries with them.

☐ asks questions	☐ honest	☐ supportive
☐ attentive	☐ loving	☐ touch
☐ attuned	☐ nonjudgmental	☐ trustworthy
☐ calls you out	☐ present	☐ validating
☐ calm	☐ reciprocity	☐ vulnerability
☐ consistent	☐ same values	☐ warm
☐ encouraging	☐ sensitive	☐ wise
☐ eye contact	☐ sets boundaries	
☐ follow-through	☐ smiling	
☐ gentle	☐ strong	

Emotions are like the weather and the sky is like the self.
Draw around and within the clouds to create a picture of the weather that best
represents how you feel when worry is moving through. Maybe it feels
like a rainstorm or like sunshine streaming through clouds. Remember: Worry is
like the weather, just passing through.

JUST BECAUSE
I FEEL AFRAID
DOESN'T MEAN
MY FEARS
ARE GOING TO
COME TRUE.

Do you express your worry? If so, how? Does expressing your worry amplify the worry or soothe it?

_____

_____

_____

_____

_____

_____

_____

_____

_____

_____

_____

Worry is a mind and body experience. When you're mindful of your thoughts, you learn to be aware of them. When you're mindful of the sensations in your body, you develop body awareness. When you can fluctuate between thoughts and sensations, you increase your mindfulness skills and your ability to choose what you focus on. You can reduce worry when you change your focus.

1. Find a quiet space to sit or lay down.

2. Close your eyes, then begin scanning your body and noting any sensations you feel that are letting you know you feel worried.

3. Allow yourself to linger with these sensations for a few minutes.

4. Bring your focus to your thoughts.

5. Listen to what worry has to say without letting your thoughts hijack you and without trying to justify, fix, or dismiss the message.

6. Make your way back to your body.

7. Notice what sensations you feel in your body and what emotions are bubbling to the surface.

8. Go back to your thoughts and listen.

9. Allow yourself to fluctuate between the body and the mind for five to ten minutes.

Gratitude is the antidote to worry. While our brains have a negativity bias, meaning they are more likely to pay attention to a threat than safety, gratitude helps counterbalance this. You have influence over what you focus on; therefore, you have the capacity to shift how you feel. Gratitude has the effect of helping you refocus on positive emotions. It guides you to take an optimistic and solution-oriented approach to obstacles you face. Write down several worries. Then, next to each one, write down something you're grateful for.

WORRY	GRATITUDE

MY FEELINGS
ARE VALID, AND
WHEN I LET
MYSELF FEEL
THEM, I AM
VALIDATING MY
EXPERIENCE.

When you see someone else who is worried, how does it make you feel? Do you experience the same feelings for, or about, yourself when you feel worried?

_____

_____

_____

_____

_____

_____

_____

_____

_____

_____

_____

_____

Take a moment to notice your body. Underneath emotions are sensations. I
n the picture, draw lines from the words to the places on the body where you feel the
sensation. Then add lines connecting the sensations to the emotions
attached to them.Learning to notice sensations will help you feel and release emotions.

EMOTIONS:

Anger

Anxiety

Calm

Fear

Joy

Sadness

Worry

SENSATIONS:

Buzzy

Fluidity

Heat

Heaviness

Lightness

Rigidity

Tension

When you feel worried, there's a tendency to lean into control. We often focus on the things we cannot control, and that only heightens worry. We need to shift the focus. First, name five things that you cannot control. For each thing you can't control, name one thing that is within your control. This will help you change what you focus on, build your confidence, and reduce your worry.

WHAT CAN'T YOU CONTROL?	WHAT CAN YOU CONTROL?

Describe the first time you remember feeling worried. Why did you feel worried? What was the result of the experience?

_____

_____

_____

_____

_____

_____

_____

_____

_____

_____

_____

Breath work is a practice that is available to you anywhere. The breath is one of your greatest tools for slowing down your mind and thoughts. But when your mind is racing and your breathing is shallow, it's not always enough to just take a deep breath. The mind also needs something to focus on.

1. Find a quiet place to sit down and close your eyes.

2. Imagine the shape of a cube in your mind's eye.

3. Inhale through your nose, and as you breathe in, imagine you are climbing up the side of the box.

4. Exhale through your nose and imagine you are sliding across the top of the box.

5. Inhale and imagine descending down the side of the box.

6. Exhale and imagine sliding across the bottom of the box.

7. Continue this exercise as many times as needed.

I TRUST THE
PROCESS AND
LET GO OF THE
OUTCOME. I AM
SAFE IN THE
HERE AND NOW.

When you catch yourself in a worry spiral, how do you feel about yourself? Do you judge and invalidate your own feelings? It's important, instead, to validate your feelings—especially the feeling of worry. Your worry is valid, even if it's not factual. It's a powerful practice to become more mindful and implement a *reframe,* or a shift in perspective, when you're making judgments about yourself. Instead of asking, "What is wrong with me?" you can reframe the question as, "What do I need?" Write down seven disempowering thoughts you have when you're worried, then reframe them.

THOUGHT	REFRAME
What's wrong with me?	What do I need?

How often do you feel worried? Is worried an emotion, or does it feel like a constant state? Does worry feel like part of your identity or personality?

_____

_____

_____

_____

_____

_____

_____

_____

_____

_____

_____

In each balloon, write down a worry that you're holding on to.
Imagine releasing the balloons that hold all of your worries. Watch the balloons float
away into the horizon. Feel your worries float away, too.

A mantra is a form of meditation that uses sounds, words, or phrases to help focus the mind.

When you feel worried, notice what you're most worried about. Name the worst-case scenario and then reframe the thought based on the best-case scenario. In order to deepen your belief that the best-case scenario is as probable, if not more probable, than the worst-case scenario, what is it that you need to hear? (For example, "I am safe.")

1. Select a mantra that feels supportive.

2. Set a timer for five minutes and find a quiet place to rest, either seated or lying down.

3. With eyes closed, repeat your mantra silently or aloud for five minutes. Each time you get distracted, come back to your mantra.

4. Notice how you feel after your mantra meditation. Notice how your focus can influence how worried you feel.

When you're not feeling worried, how do you feel? What is the opposite of worried?

_____

_____

_____

_____

_____

_____

_____

_____

_____

_____

_____

Experiencing worry is normal. Excessive worry isn't. Excessive worry can feel out of control and unsafe. You have felt worried for so long that you don't know what it feels like to be emotionally safe. To feel safe, you need grounding practices, self-soothing tools, and connection to people you feel comfortable with.

What does safety feel like in your body? Circle all that apply.

Alone	Exposed	Present
Buzzy	Free	Protected
Calm	Hidden	Relaxed
Clear	Light	Tense
Connected	Openhearted	Vulnerable
Disconnected	Open-minded	

What is weighing heavily on your mind? Write these thoughts on the stones to release the weight you've been carrying. Imagine tossing the stones to the bottom of a lake. You don't have to carry the weight of these thoughts any longer.

When do you feel most at peace? Describe who you're with and what you are doing. How could you create more space in your current routine for more of this?

_____

_____

_____

_____

_____

_____

_____

_____

_____

_____

_____

_____

The psoas muscle connects the upper and lower body, weaving through the hip joint and connecting to the lower back. The psoas has been called "the muscle of the soul" because it's connected to our emotions and to our survival instincts.

When the psoas is tight and constricted, it's signaling danger to the body. The contraction is meant to recoil energy, to contain it, until it's time to flee, fight, or freeze. Flight, fight, and freeze are your survival instincts in response to danger.

When you feel worried, you're sensing danger. While you may be looking for the danger outside yourself, it's often coming from trauma stored inside your body. Trauma constricts the psoas.

To free yourself from worry, the psoas needs to be released.

1. When you become aware that you're feeling worried, find a comfortable place to stand with your feet wider than hip distance apart.

2. Place your hands on your hips and begin making hip circles, as if you had a Hula-Hoop around your waist.

3. Allow this gentle movement to stretch the front side of your body, open your psoas muscle, and gently soothe the nervous system.

Worry is "what if" oriented. With worry, there is a sense of impending doom, and the what-ifs can feel endless. However scary the unknown may feel, there are knowns in the present moment: the "what is." Learning to focus the mind on "what is" will short-circuit worry. Fill in each blank to reframe a "what-if" into "what is" and notice how your worry reduces.

What if _____

What is _____

What if _____

What is _____

What if _____

What is _____

What if _____

What is _____

What if _____

What is _____

What are you most grateful for in this moment? Draw or write about it in the gift image.

Worry is a survival strategy. How has worry attempted to protect you?

_____

_____

_____

_____

_____

_____

_____

_____

_____

_____

_____

Worry gets unmanageable when you are alone in it and let it fester in your mind. Although we don't always have someone to share with in person, we can still share our worries out loud.

1. Grab your phone and open up the voice memo app.

2. Put on a timer for ten minutes and hit record. The app represents a container to place all your worries in. It's here so that you can unburden all your worries by speaking them aloud.

3. Start speaking whenever you are ready. You don't have to say the right thing or say it perfectly; you just need to start sharing what's on your mind.

4. When the ten minutes are up, notice how you feel. You may feel a lot lighter, like you got something off your chest. You may also have discovered some new insights about how you feel and what you need to feel less worried.

When you feel worried, often you're also judging your feelings. To practice awareness without judgment, take a seat by a window. Notice everything you see from this vantage point. Instead of labeling the nouns you see, practice noticing colors, patterns, shapes, sizes, movement, and textures. Write down what you notice through observation without labels and awareness without fixation. This will help you let go of your judgments around worry.

What do you see outside the window?

_____

_____

_____

_____

_____

_____

_____

_____

_____

Our beliefs shape our reality. Do you believe things happen *to* you or *for* you? What do you believe you have control over?

_____

_____

_____

_____

_____

_____

_____

_____

_____

_____

_____

Where does your worry come from?
Having a clear story helps you organize your self-understanding and supports
ongoing growth. Think back to your childhood. Were the adults in your
life worriers? What did they worry about? Write or draw the worries around the figure.

Sometimes we experience feelings about our feelings, known as secondary emotions. What judgments do you have of yourself when you feel worried? How do you feel about yourself when you're worried?

_____

_____

_____

_____

_____

_____

_____

_____

_____

_____

_____

When you react from a place of worry, it's usually involuntary. It just happens. You might feel out of control. Then you might regret how you reacted, causing even more worry. To take back control of how you respond to worry, it's helpful to be more intentional and take time to respond rather than impulsively reacting. Name five ways that you have reacted when you felt worried in the past. Then identify five ways you can intentionally respond when you feel worried in the future. These voluntary, or chosen, responses will help you create a greater sense of control and lead to more peace.

INVOLUNTARY RESPONSE	INTENTIONAL RESPONSE

Imagine a place that makes you feel safe. Write a brief description of this place in the smallest circle. In the next circle, describe what qualities this place has that make you feel safe. In the outermost circle, describe what safety feels like.

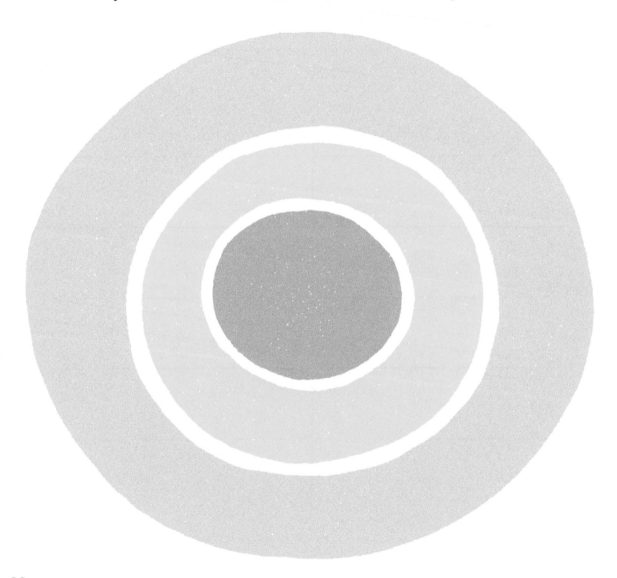

Yoga is a practice that brings you back into your body and out of your head. Not only does it help you feel more flexible, but it also helps you learn to find stillness in chaos. Worry definitely feels like chaos.

1. Find space on the floor and roll out a yoga mat or towel.

2. Set a timer for ten minutes.

3. Lay flat on your back, then bring your hands to your stomach and allow your legs to stretch out in front of you.

4. Bring the soles of your feet together so they are touching and let your knees open wide.

5. Rest within this relaxing posture.

6. Take deep breaths and notice if your knees gradually open wider as your body relaxes and softens.

7. Notice how chaos can ease into peace.

When you feel worried, are you focusing on the past, present, or future? What helps you feel more present?

_____

_____

_____

_____

_____

_____

_____

_____

_____

_____

Behind worry is a fear of what is going to happen in the future. When you're worrying about the future, you're overpreparing for every possible worst-case scenario. Instead of continuing to catastrophize, examine the fear. Name the first fear that comes to mind. Ask yourself why you fear this. Continue asking until you get to the root fear. Then ask if you could live with that.

FEAR	
WHY DO YOU FEAR THIS?	
WHY DO YOU FEAR THIS?	
WHY DO YOU FEAR THIS?	
WHY DO YOU FEAR THIS?	
ROOT FEAR	
COULD YOU LIVE WITH THIS?	

If worry was a small child, what would they need from their parent to feel a sense of calm? How would their parent comfort them? Write down what both the parent and child would say.

Has worry ever led you to self-sabotage? What happened? Do you hold any regrets?

_____

_____

_____

_____

_____

_____

_____

_____

_____

_____

_____

When you feel worried, you're off-balance. The mind and body are often on different pages, and it's difficult to find your center. It's hard to come back to the present moment when you feel worried.

When you become aware that you feel worried, you have the opportunity to restabilize.

1. When you are aware of feeling worried, find enough space where you can stand comfortably and move around.

2. Set a timer for 60 seconds and begin to balance on one leg.

3. Repeat this exercise on the other side of the body.

4. Take a moment to notice how it feels to focus so intently on the body and balancing.

5. Repeat the activity up to five times on each side and note how it shifts your worry and brings you back to embodiment in the present moment.

When you feel worried, notice how many times your inner dialogue starts
with the words "I should." Write your "shoulds" on the water droplets. Let your "shoulds"
wash away. Notice how your worries ease into more peace.

Worry is a universal human experience. Excessive worry is not. Excessive worry is debilitating and often leads to anxiety. It's important to be able to identify the difference within yourself so you can support yourself. Make a check mark next to the symptoms you experience to gain more awareness of the level of worry you're experiencing. Tally how many check marks you make in each column to identify if you're struggling with excessive worry.

WORRY	EXCESSIVE WORRY
Racing heart	Rumination
Nausea	Digestive problems
Headache	Overthinking
In your head	Obsessing
Emotional eating	Weight gain or weight loss
Irritation	Rage
Lack of motivation	Anxiety or depression

Write a letter to your worry. Express the range of emotions you feel toward worry. Let worry know what you think.

_____

_____

_____

_____

_____

_____

_____

_____

_____

_____

_____

You may have heard the quote "Worry is a conversation you have with yourself about things you cannot control." How can you make this conversation more productive? Use words or pictures to show how the conversation could guide you out of worry.

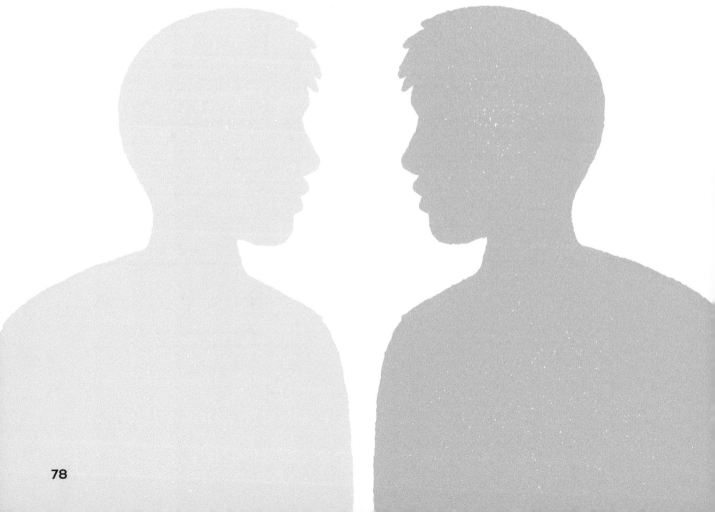

Underneath emotions are sensations that are alive in the body. What does worry feel like in your body? Where do you feel worry in your body?

_____

_____

_____

_____

_____

_____

_____

_____

_____

_____

_____

_____

The nervous system determines if you feel worried or not. The central nervous system is housed within the spinal cord and extends to the brain and throughout the whole body. By settling the nervous system, you can ease your worries.

1. To help your nervous system transition from worry to calm, find a quiet place to sit where you can close your eyes and feel supported below and behind you.

2. Bring one hand to the base of the skull and the other hand to the lower stomach, touching both ends of the nervous system.

3. Take a few rounds of breath here to settle into stillness.

4. On the next breath, inhale through your nose for a count of four, hold the inhale at the top for a count of four, and slowly exhale through the nose for a count of eight, pausing on empty for a count of four.

5. Repeat for ten rounds of breath.

6. Feel your breath through the rise and fall of your stomach and notice the support and comfort you feel from the touch of your hands. Notice how you have settled your nervous system and eased your worry.

Whatever you resist will persist. This rule applies to worry as well. If you try to resist it, suppress it, or ignore it, it will fester. What you can do, however, is bring curiosity to your worries. Resistance feels rigid in the body, but curiosity brings a softening. You're saying to yourself that you are open to understanding rather than judging. What are five questions you could ask your worry that would expand your curiosity?

1. _____

2. _____

3. _____

4. _____

5. _____

Imagine releasing all your self-doubts. What insecurities are weighing
you down and preventing you from being free? Write your doubts and insecurities in the
leaves and watch as they fall to the ground.

What would it be like if you had a relationship with your worry? If you made space to listen to what worry had to say instead of trying to silence it? Instead of trying to get rid of worry, could you coexist with it?

_____

_____

_____

_____

_____

_____

_____

_____

_____

_____

_____

It's time to face your worry in order to understand it more fully. Understanding gives you more clarity about what will help you feel more peace. Fill in the blanks with the first thought that comes to mind. There is no right answer. This exercise will help you learn more about your experience with worry.

When I'm worried, I'm _____.

If I'm worried, something is _____.

Worry means _____.

Everyone will _____ when I'm worried.

Worry makes me feel _____.

When I'm worried, I want _____.

When I'm worried, I need _____.

No one _____ when I'm worried.

When I'm worried, I can _____.

Worry serves _____ purpose.

I am _____ when I don't feel worried.

Understanding the vagus nerve will help you work with your nervous system rather than against it. The vagus nerve is not only the longest nerve in the body, but it also connects your brain to other vital organs, including the gut, heart, and lungs. It influences breathing, heart rate, and digestive function. It's important to have a high vagal tone, which means your body can relax faster after stress. When you have a higher vagal tone, you have quicker access to relaxation and recovery.

The next time you feel worried, try finishing your shower with 30 seconds of cold water. Over time, gradually increase your cold water exposure in the shower, up to a few minutes. Notice and track how frequent cold exposure decreases your worry.

What habits do you need to abandon in order to feel less worried? What behaviors contribute to your sense of worry?

_____

_____

_____

_____

_____

_____

_____

_____

_____

_____

The next time you feel worried, remember you have the tools to find peace again. What are your top five tools that you can keep handy to use the next time you feel worried? Just remembering you have them will help you feel calmer.

Sensations in the body are different from emotions. Sensations give language to how the body feels physically. When you develop body awareness, you become more connected to your intuition and instincts, and more confident that you will be okay when faced with obstacles that used to make you worry. In the chart, describe sensations you feel when you have experiences that are uncomfortable, neutral, and pleasurable. Expanding your vocabulary to describe how your body feels will also expand your body awareness and capacity to soothe yourself when you feel worried.

UNCOMFORTABLE	NEUTRAL	PLEASURABLE
Tension	Hair resting on my shoulders	Lightness

How has worry impacted your life? How would your life be different if you worried less?

_____

_____

_____

_____

_____

_____

_____

_____

_____

_____

_____

_____

Journaling is a practice that helps you see yourself more clearly. It allows you to dump excess thoughts, noise, and worry outside yourself.

Often when we journal, we go on tangents, ending up somewhere we didn't see coming. This is the beauty of letting go. Sometimes we have to clear the noise out of the way so we can go deeper into the self.

1. Find a quiet place.

2. Light a candle.

3. Turn on soothing music.

4. Grab your favorite pen.

5. Set a timer for ten minutes and let yourself write. Try to write for the full ten minutes without lifting your pen from the paper. This will allow everything that needs to come forward to be put down on paper so you don't have to carry it around anymore.

To help prevent worry, you need tools as well as practices. Tools help you cope in moments of worry, while practices are experiences you create regularly. Checking in with yourself and how you're feeling, noticing sensations in your body, and witnessing your thoughts are practices you can cultivate. With that in mind, answer the following check-in questions:

How does my energy feel? _____

Is there tension or lack of tension in my body? _____

How much of me (percentage) is present and how much of me isn't? _____

How deep or shallow is my breath? _____

What do I need right now to feel my best? _____

Think of your biggest dream, the one that worry tries to talk you out of.
Write it on the dartboard. On each dart, write a strength that you already have that will
continue to direct you toward your biggest dreams.

What you resist persists. To surrender is to cease resistance. How can you surrender to your worry so that you can feel more at peace?

_____

_____

_____

_____

_____

_____

_____

_____

_____

_____

_____

When you feel worried, you feel stuck because your emotions are stuck. To unstick emotions, they need to be felt and expressed. Sensations begin in the stomach and turn into emotions in the heart. Emotions are released when expressed from the throat. Name five sensations, emotions, thoughts, and ways that you could express your worry to get unstuck.

SENSATION IN THE STOMACH	EMOTION IN THE HEART	THOUGHT RUNNING THROUGH YOUR MIND	EXPRESSION FROM THE THROAT

Worry makes your body and mind feel disconnected. Worry isn't part of your natural rhythm. It drains your energy while making you feel strung out.

Authentic movement has the capacity to bring your body and mind back into their natural rhythm. There is no right way to dance; there is only movement that comes authentically out of you.

1. Turn on music that you enjoy.

2. Pick one song and commit to moving for the entire song.

The movement will release tension in your body and release feel-good hormones to combat worry. Dance will invite your body back into rhythm.

If your best friend was feeling worried, what advice would you give them? How would you offer support? Do you offer the same advice and support to yourself?

_____

_____

_____

_____

_____

_____

_____

_____

_____

_____

_____

Within every challenge there is also an opportunity. You've been through hard things and have overcome them. Think about a particularly challenging experience you've been through. In the open field, draw or write what you learned from it.

Worry is your imagination being used against you. If you can imagine worst-case scenarios, then you can imagine best-case scenarios, too. In the chart provided, write down the worst-case scenario and the best-case scenario for four situations. Notice how each of the possible outcomes makes you feel. Choose the one that feels the most empowering.

WORST-CASE SCENARIO	BEST-CASE SCENARIO

Worry is excess energy trapped in the body, and exercise can move and release this energy.

1. Choose an exercise based on your level of fitness and mobility, such as squats, squat jumps, planks, push-ups, high knees, jumping jacks, or mountain climbers. Make modifications as needed.

2. Perform your exercise for twenty seconds, then rest for ten seconds.

3. Do this rotation eight times, or for four minutes total.

4. Notice how you feel before and after the exercise.

Gradually work up to repeating three rounds of the four-minute exercise interval and experiment with different movement patterns. Not only will you expend some of your worry energy, but you will also receive a hit of feel-good hormones.

Your body is your home. In the picture of the house, describe the elements of your "home"—the structure, foundation, and exterior. What part needs the most TLC?

Can you identify a trigger before you feel worried? Do you notice a pattern between your triggers and when you feel worried?

_____

_____

_____

_____

_____

_____

_____

_____

_____

_____

_____

Negative thinking is part of what makes worry uncomfortable, but with awareness, you can stop negative thoughts in their tracks and replace them with positive thoughts. Make a list of five negative thoughts that go through your mind. Then, create two believable, positive stories for each negative thought. Focusing on the positive thoughts will help you change the habit of negative thinking. At first it takes practice, but before you know it, it becomes an organic process.

NEGATIVE THOUGHT	POSITIVE STORY	POSITIVE STORY

We need to create boundaries with others, ourselves,
and our emotions. Imagine boundaries as a fence that offers protection.
Draw what your fence looks like around the house.

When you feel worried, you breathe in more than you breathe out.

You need not be a professional singer to use the simple practice of singing or chanting to influence the breath. When you sing, your exhales naturally lengthen, matching your inhales.

1. Turn on a song that you know all the lyrics to.

2. Put the song on repeat.

3. Turn up the volume.

4. Sing like no one is listening.

Singing will balance out your breath and bring more movement into your jaw, more mobility into your body, and more freedom from the sensations of worry.

The feeling of urgency is present when you're worried. You think you have to have it all figured out and act immediately. Sometimes action is needed, and sometimes patience is needed more. Bring more awareness to the feeling of urgency and answer the following questions.

What does urgency feel like in your body? _____

_____

Have you felt this sense of urgency before? _____

_____

When you've acted out of urgency in the past, has it been helpful or hurtful?

_____

_____

Was this situation as urgent as it felt? _____

_____

What would change if you brought in more patience? _____

_____

When has being patient paid off? _____

_____

When you feel worried, how old do you feel? What does this version of yourself need to hear to help soothe the worry?

_____

_____

_____

_____

_____

_____

_____

_____

_____

_____

_____

_____

_____

Sometimes when you feel worried, you need an ally to help you ease
the discomfort. An ally can be a being or person in your life, such as an animal, ancestor,
or spiritual figure. Imagine the figure below is your ally. Use words or pictures
to show what your ally has to share with you.

When worry gets to be too much, you might find yourself avoiding the people or places that make you feel worried. You might not even be aware of all that you're avoiding in an effort to not feel worried. Although this is a good temporary strategy, eventually your world begins to shrink as your avoidance expands. To change the trajectory, it's helpful to identify the places you're avoiding and intentionally expose yourself to them in small amounts. It will also help to have a self-care plan as you approach what you've been avoiding. Fill out the following chart.

WHAT/WHO ARE YOU AVOIDING?	HOW CAN YOU APPROACH THIS PLACE/PERSON IN A SMALL WAY?	WHAT SELF-CARE TOOL WILL SUPPORT YOU BEFORE, DURING, OR AFTER EXPOSURE?

Write down the first thoughts that run through your mind when you're worried. Do you notice that the same thoughts repeat each time you feel worried? If the same thoughts are repeating, does that make them more or less likely to come true?

_____

_____

_____

_____

_____

_____

_____

_____

_____

_____

_____

When you feel worried, it's a signal to do less, not more. Worry indicates that you're in need of rest, not productivity.

Nature is the greatest teacher for slowing down and returning to your natural rhythm. Nature doesn't hurry, isn't easily controlled, and offers a sense of expansion.

Let worry be an invitation to be in nature and connect to the earth. Take yourself somewhere outside where you can take your shoes off and put your bare feet on the earth—somewhere you can soak in thirty minutes of sunshine and vitamin D (vitamin D helps to regulate mood). Notice how your worry decreases when you give yourself permission to slow down and reconnect.

Daily habits have the potential to create noticeable change, growth, and healing. Daily habits are intentional practices that focus on shifting your mindset and mood. One daily habit that works to this end involves regularly gauging how you feel and figuring out what you need to feel your best. Ask yourself the following questions each morning to begin forming this habit.

What are my intentions today? _____

What am I grateful for today?_____

How do I want to feel today? _____

What do I love about myself today? _____

Worry and control often go hand in hand. When you feel
worried, you hold on tightly to things, people, and beliefs. When you feel calm, you
relax your grip and allow things to just be. What are you holding on to?
What can you let rest in your open palm? Use words or pictures to fill the hand.

Worry is just energy. You have the capacity to manage your energy and, therefore, manage your worries. Sometimes you need to slow down to manage your energy—be still and quiet, and rest. Other times you need movement, exercise, and action. It's important to know how to influence your energy so you can ease your worries. In the chart, name five practices (such as journaling) that will help you slow down, and name five more practices (such as going for a walk) that are geared toward action.

STILLNESS PRACTICES	MOVEMENT EXERCISES

There is a connection between the breath and the pelvic floor, yet many people are disconnected from this part of their body. When you take a deep breath, the muscles in the pelvic floor, located between your pubic bone and tailbone, lengthen a little bit. When you breathe out, they contract.

1. Lie on your back with a pillow under your head and under your knees.

2. Breathe in gently through your nose.

3. Bring your awareness to your pelvic floor muscles.

4. As you breathe out, engage the pelvic floor by imagining you're stopping the flow of urine.

5. When you inhale, relax your pelvic floor.

6. Notice how the length of your breath is connected to an ease in worry.

7. Repeat as needed.

Worry serves a purpose. How is worry serving you? What meaning do you assign to worry?

_____

_____

_____

_____

_____

_____

_____

_____

_____

_____

_____

_____

Imagine yourself as a flower. When you're feeling worried,
you're like a tight bud. When you're feeling peaceful and joyful, you unfold.
Use the flower petals to write or draw how you feel when you are open.

Although there are a lot of things in life you cannot control, there are always things you can, such as how you respond. Sometimes it's hard to remember this when you are caught in a worry spiral. In the space below, name ten things you can control. The next time you feel worried, remind yourself of what you can control in that moment.

1. _____

2. _____

3. _____

4. _____

5. _____

6. _____

7. _____

8. _____

9. _____

10. _____

Learning how to slow down helps you trust the process rather than worrying about the outcome. How do you feel when you focus on the outcome? How do you feel when you focus on the process?

_____

_____

_____

_____

_____

_____

_____

_____

_____

_____

_____

_____

If your best friend was feeling worried, how would you comfort them?
Write a letter to yourself showing the same kindness you would show to your best friend
and read it the next time you feel worried.

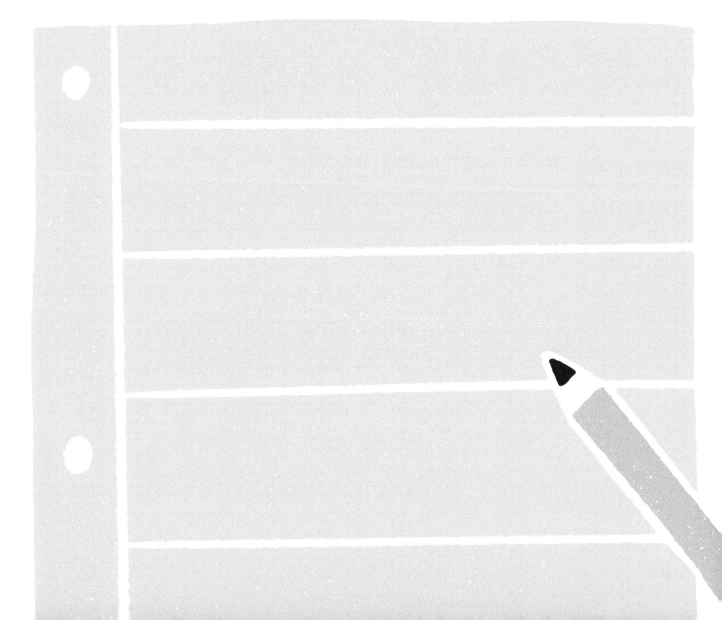

When do you feel your absolute best? When do you feel energized and grounded? What habits and practices support this feeling?

_____

_____

_____

_____

_____

_____

_____

_____

_____

_____

_____

You need to feel safe to ease your worries, but sometimes you may not have access to a safe person or place. You can, however, use the power of the imagination to provoke feelings of safety. Imagine a person or a place that makes you feel calm and relaxed. While imagining this person or place, bring awareness to all your senses and describe what you notice.

PERSON/PLACE	
WHAT DO YOU SEE?	
WHAT DO YOU SMELL?	
WHAT DO YOU HEAR?	
WHAT DO YOU TASTE?	
WHAT DO YOU FEEL OR TOUCH?	

Imagine one of the books pictured represents the past, one the present, and one the future. Give each book a title that signifies what the past, present, and future each mean to you. The next time you feel worried, imagine picking up the book about the present to help you come back to the moment.

The vagus nerve facilitates communication between the mind and body. One point of connection for the vagus nerve is the vocal cords and muscles in the back of your throat. By stimulating the vagus nerve, you can send a message to your body that it's okay to relax and de-stress.

The next time you feel worried, take the following steps to stimulate the vagus nerve:

1. Pour a large glass of water.

2. Take a sip and gargle the water in the back of your throat.

3. Repeat step 2 until you have finished your glass of water.

A resilient nervous system can move back and forth between worry and calm. Answer the questions below as you move back and forth between these two states.

When you are feeling worried, notice how you feel physically.

Where do you feel the worry? _____

What does it feel like?_____

Now scan your body and find a place that feels neutral or relaxed. Stay with that feeling for

a moment, really giving yourself time to experience it.

Where do you feel relaxed? _____

What does it feel like?_____

Continue this process, shifting your attention between these two areas of your body slowly.

Stay with the worry and allow yourself to really experience it. Then, shift your attention back

to the part of your body where you don't feel worry.

As you continue to move from worried to relaxed, notice how the worry changes.

How did the worry change? _____

_____

_____

When you're worried, do you feel like you're more in your head or more in your body? Do your mind and body feel like they're on the same page or telling different stories? What are their stories?

_____

_____

_____

_____

_____

_____

_____

_____

_____

_____

_____

_____

Bring your hands to your stomach and take a deep breath.
Feel the rise and fall of your breath and the quiet that settles in your body and mind.
It's from this place of quiet that you can hear the voice of your intuition.
What does your intuition say that you need in this moment? Use words or pictures
to show what your voice is saying.

Resilience is about how quickly you can recover from difficulties. Worry is about preparing for possible difficulties. Is there a connection between resilience and worry?

_____

_____

_____

_____

_____

_____

_____

_____

_____

_____

_____

_____

Every person has many layers and parts to them that make up who they are as a whole. We carry younger versions of ourselves around with us. Each part has different needs and has its own unique voice. In the chart, identify five parts of you. When you become aware of these parts, you can learn what their needs are and what they're trying to tell you.

PART	Inner Child	Inner Teenager	Inner Mother	Inner Father	Inner Critic
GIVE THIS PART A NAME.					
WHAT DOES THIS PART NEED?					
WHAT IS THIS PART TRYING TO TELL YOU?					
WHAT OR WHO IS THIS PART TRYING TO PROTECT?					
WHAT EMTIONS AND THOUGHTS DOES THIS PART FEEL?					

Before there is excessive worry, there is worry. Can you spot the
signs of worry so you can implement self-care before it becomes excessive? Write
down the progressive signs in the ladder provided and how
you can soothe yourself at each step to discourage escalation.

Do you feel safe when you feel worried? Do you feel safer when you're alone and worried, or when you're with another person? Why?

_____

_____

_____

_____

_____

_____

_____

_____

_____

_____

_____

The amount of worry you feel isn't correlated to the reality of your fears coming true, even when it feels like it. Worrying also doesn't prevent or protect you from your fears coming true. When you feel worried, you're actually less present with what's right in front of you, your body, your intuition, and your environment. It's helpful to fact-check your worried thoughts so that you can be more present and let them go. Choose a thought you have when you're feeling worried, and fact-check it.

WORRY THOUGHT	
IS THIS TRUE?	
HAS THIS HAPPENED BEFORE?	
DID I SURVIVE?	
WHAT'S THE WORST-CASE SCENARIO?	
WILL I BE OKAY?	

Bring your hands to your heart and take a deep breath.
What message is within your heart that you need to hear in this moment?
Write or draw it in the space provided. Breathe deeply into this message.

RESOURCES

The following resources offer continued support for reducing and letting go of worry. Since worry encompasses many different emotions and symptom manifestations, you will find a range of topics, to support your healing, including help for trauma and anxiety. Worry isn't specific to a demographic; therefore, resources have been included to support children and adults with reducing worry. The continued support will offer further creative, mind and body, explorative tools to help you leave worry in the past.

The Anxiety & Worry Workbook: The Cognitive Behavioral Solution by David A. Clark and Aaron T. Beck

Anxiety: The Missing Stage of Grief: A Revolutionary Approach to Understanding and Healing the Impact of Loss by Claire Bidwell Smith

Big Magic: Creative Living Beyond Fear by Elizabeth Gilbert

Mind Over Mood, Second Edition: Change How You Feel by Changing the Way You Think by Dennis Greenberger and Christine A. Padesky

The Surrender Experiment: My Journey into Life's Perfection by Michael A. Singer

Unfuck Your Brain: Using Science to Get Over Anxiety, Depression, Anger, Freak-Outs, and Triggers by Faith G. Harper

Unwinding Anxiety: New Science Shows How to Break the Cycles of Worry and Fear to Heal Your Mind by Judson Brewer

Waking the Tiger: Healing Trauma by Peter A. Levine

What to Do When You Worry Too Much: A Kid's Guide to Overcoming Anxiety by Dawn Huebner

When Things Fall Apart: Heart Advice for Difficult Times by Pema Chödrön

Acknowledgments

I would like to thank Vanessa Putt for her time and interest in recruiting me to write this journal, Mary Colgan for her editorial genius and elegant way of delivering feedback, and the entire team at Callisto Media for their dedicated research and unique style of publishing that supports authors in bringing needed work out into the world. Gratitude to my teachers, Peter Levine, Carl Jung, and Stephen Porges, and my mentors, Amy Doublet and Trish Lange, all who have supported my growth and understanding of holistic well-being.

About the Author

 **Erika Straub,** MA, BA, RYT, is an international trauma and anxiety coach, writer, and speaker. She holds a bachelor's and master's in psychology. Her work with clients is informed by the modalities of Polyvagal Theory, Somatic Experiencing, Attachment Theory, Internal Family Systems, and Jungian Depth Psychology. Erika specializes in nervous system regulation and repairing attachment wounds. Erika believes trauma healing is a spiritual experience that invites you back into connection with self, others, and source.

Erika is also a professional equestrian and avid traveler, and resides in Los Angeles, California.

To learn more about Erika, visit AnxiousFemale.com or follow her on Instagram @_anxiousfemale.